ISAAC ASIMOV'S
Library of the Universe
MERCURY:
The Quick Planet

by Isaac Asimov

Gareth Stevens Publishing
Milwaukee

Library of Congress Cataloging-in-Publication Data

Asimov, Isaac, 1920-
    Mercury, the quick planet.

    (Isaac Asimov's library of the universe)
    Bibliography: p.
    Includes index.
    Summary: Describes the characteristics of the small planet closest to the sun
whose day is twice as long as its year.
    1. Mercury (Planet)—Juvenile literature. [1. Mercury (Planet)] I. Title. II.
Series: Asimov, Isaac, 1920-   . Library of the universe.
QB611.A75   1989   523.41   87-42605
ISBN 1-55532-360-X

A Gareth Stevens Children's Books edition

Edited, designed, and produced by
Gareth Stevens, Inc. 7317 West Green Tree Road Milwaukee, Wisconsin 53223, USA

Cover painting © Rick Sternbach
Project editor: Mark Sachner
Designer: Laurie Shock
Research editor: Scott Enk
Picture research: Matthew Groshek
Technical advisers and consulting editors: Julian Baum and Francis Reddy

9931

1 2 3 4 5 6 7 8 9 94 93 92 91 90 89

Printed in the United States of America

CONTENTS

Nowadays, we have seen planets up close, all the way to distant Uranus. We have mapped Venus through its clouds. We have seen dead volcanoes on Mars and live ones on Io, one of Jupiter's satellites. We have detected strange objects no one knew anything about until recently: quasars, pulsars, black holes. We have learned amazing facts about how the Universe was born and have some ideas about how it may die. Nothing can be more astonishing and more interesting.

One of the planets we have seen up close is Mercury, which is the nearest planet to the Sun. It is so near the Sun that it is usually overwhelmed by the Sun's light when we try to see it. That is one reason why until recently we knew very little about Mercury. That is changed now. We have learned quite a bit, and in this book we will try to explain our new knowledge of this small, quick planet.

Isaac Asimov

The Silent Fire

Mercury is a small planet — at 3,030 miles (4,875 km) across, it is only three-eighths the width of Earth. It is the closest planet to the Sun — only 36 million miles (57.9 million km) away on the average. And it comes as close as 29 million miles (46.6 million km) as it orbits the Sun. This is almost 70% closer to the Sun than Earth is.

The surface of any planet this close to the Sun is bound to get very hot — as hot as 660°F (348°C), which is hot enough to melt lead. And since Mercury is so close to the Sun, the Sun's gravity pulls hard. Earth moves about the Sun at 18.6 miles (29.9 km) a second, but Mercury moves at an average of 29.8 miles (47.9 km) a second. It is the quick planet.

Opposite: the planet Mercury as seen by the Mariner 10 spacecraft in 1974. Its rough, cratered surface resembles that of our Moon.

Right: Glowing streams of molten metal pour into molds at a foundry. The surface of Mercury gets hot enough to melt lead.

The Two-year Day and Other Orbital Oddities

From our point of view here on Earth, Mercury has a strange relationship with the Sun. First of all, its closeness to the Sun gives it a small orbit. It moves so quickly that its trip around the Sun — its year — takes only 88 days. But Mercury turns very slowly on its <u>axis</u>, so the time from sunrise to sunrise — one Mercury day — is 176 Earth days. So Mercury's "day" is twice as long as its year!

Mercury turns on its axis with a steady speed, but its orbit is lopsided, and when it is nearer the Sun it moves faster. For that reason, the Sun moves across Mercury's sky unevenly. In fact, from certain places on Mercury, you might see the Sun rise, then set (as though it had changed its mind), and then rise again! The same would go for sunset, too — first the Sun would set, then rise briefly, and then set again.

Opposite: daytime on Mercury. Space suits would have to withstand extreme heat and cold on a planet bathed in bright sunlight and deep shadows.

Below: In this illustration, the bright yellow area of Mercury's tipped, lopsided orbit lies <u>above</u> Earth's orbital plane (shown in blue). The pink area lies <u>below</u> Earth's orbital plane. A red line shows the 7° tilt between the two orbital planes.

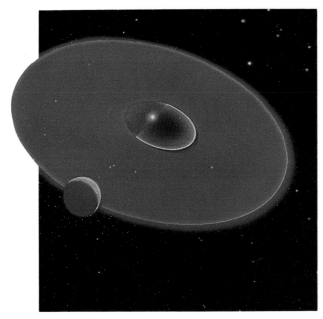

Mercury — why the wacky orbit?

Mercury's orbit is more elliptical, or lopsided, than any planetary orbit except Pluto's. Mercury's orbit is also more tipped against the general plane of planetary orbits than any orbit except Pluto's. Actually, since Mercury is so near the Sun, astronomers might think its orbit should be nearly circular and in the plane of the Sun's equator, like the orbit of Venus, the next closest planet to the Sun. Why isn't this so in Mercury's case? We don't know.

Mercury — The Inside Story

When the Solar system formed, the material outside the Sun formed vast crowds of small bodies. These small bodies gradually crashed into each other and formed larger bodies. The gravitational pull of the larger bodies attracted most remaining small bodies, and so the planets formed.

Very close to the Sun, the lighter material all boiled away. Mercury formed only out of rocks and metal — materials that have a very high melting point. Mercury is therefore second only to Earth in density. Like Venus and Earth, Mercury has a large metallic center. But of all the known planets in our Solar system, Mercury's metallic center seems to be the largest for its size.

Mercury's building blocks were rock and metal fragments that formed close to the Sun.

Beneath Mercury's Sun-baked surface lies a large central core of metal.

The negatives and positives of Mercury's magnetic field

Earth and at least three of the four giant planets have magnetic fields. To have a magnetic field, a planet must have a liquid center that conducts electricity, and it must rotate swiftly so that it sets the liquid swirling. The Moon and Mars do not have liquid centers, so they have no magnetic fields. Mercury rotates very slowly, so it shouldn't have a magnetic field. But it does. It has a weak magnetic field, and astronomers can't figure out why.

The Cooling Surface of a Hot Planet

When a world forms, the last few bits that strike it leave huge craters where they hit the surface. If the world is like Earth, its water and atmosphere wear down these craters and make most disappear. If the world has volcanic action, the lava from the volcanoes covers the surface and, again, most craters disappear.

Small worlds like Mercury usually don't have atmospheres or volcanic activity, so the marks left by the final collisions remain. We can see many craters on Earth's Moon, for example. Mercury, meanwhile, is so hot that its surface remained soft longer. It is even more thickly covered with craters than the Moon!

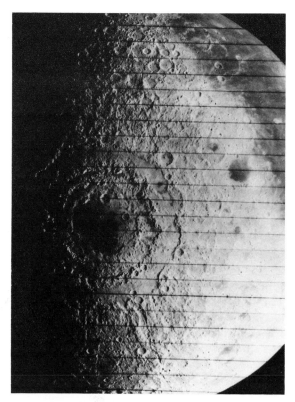

Left: Both Mercury and our Moon share the scars of collisions. The Moon's Mare Orientale impact site looks very much like a similar basin on Mercury. On the Moon, though, we can still see where lava flows later smoothed over the surface.

Opposite: Craters and bright "rays" of debris crowd Mercury's south polar area. Inset: an artist's concept of heavily cratered Mercury.

Caloris bull's-eye! The object that made this 800-mile- (1,280-km-) wide impact basin also formed a series of circular ridges.

Mercury — A Tortured Landscape

If we were to see Mercury as closely as we see the Moon, it would look very much like the Moon. It is thickly covered with craters that look somewhat smaller than those on the Moon. But that is only because Mercury is a larger body, so its craters look smaller by comparison.

We call Mercury's largest crater Caloris (meaning "heat") because it happens to have the highest temperatures on Mercury. Caloris is about 810 miles (1,300 km) across. There are also cliffs and fissures that pass right across the craters. This may be because Mercury shrank as it slowly cooled, and the surface of the planet cracked.

An artist imagines the Caloris impact.

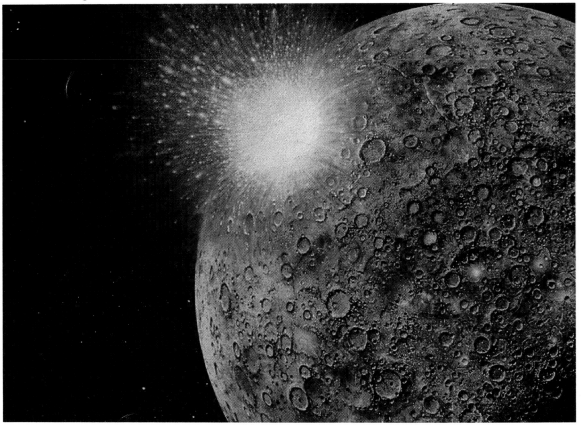

Mapping Mercury

Mercury has long been a mystery to Earthbound sky-watchers. In fact, until 1974, we didn't know anything about Mercury's surface. All we could see through a telescope was a small body near the Sun with vague shadows on it that went through phases, like the Moon and Venus.

But on November 3, 1973, scientists launched a space probe, Mariner 10, that would change our understanding of Mercury. Less than five months later — on March 29, 1974 — Mariner passed within 168.4 miles (271 km) of Mercury's surface. Then, as it went around the Sun, Mariner visited Mercury twice more, coming as close as 203 miles (327 km). It sent back detailed pictures of almost half of Mercury's surface.

Everything we know about the surface comes from those pictures. No other craft has been sent to Mercury since.

Opposite: Mariner 10 scanned Mercury's surface three times in 1974 and 1975, returning the pictures to Earth by radio beams.

Two views of Mercury. Left: the cracked floor of the Caloris basin. Right: a rugged, cratered landscape.

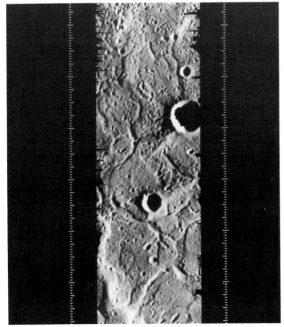 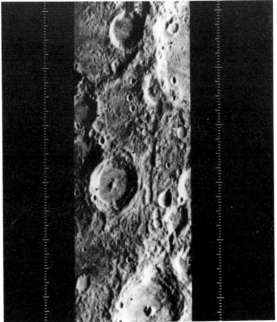

Piloted Missions to Mercury

Human beings have landed on the Moon, and plans are being made to send astronauts to Mars. But will we ever send human beings to Mercury? It might be useful to do this so we can study Mercury's surface up close.

But would it be possible to go to a planet with temperatures as hot as Mercury's? Perhaps. After all, any spot on Mercury is turned away from the Sun for 88 days at a time, so the temperature cools off rapidly. In fact, it actually gets very cold — as low as −270°F (−168°C) — during Mercury's long night. So people with the right equipment might be able to remain on the surface during the night. But approaching the Sun to get to Mercury would be quite difficult — not just because of the heat, but because of the intense ultraviolet light, x-rays, and other radiation.

Sunrise on Mercury.

Left: Astronauts on Mercury examine surface rocks for useful minerals.

Below: Thick-walled buildings made from Mercury's rocks could protect human visitors from the Sun's deadly radiation.

Left: Mercury passes between Earth and the Sun. These drawings are based on observations made in 1960. Inset: The full disk of the Sun. Mercury is the tiny black dot near bottom center.

Exploring Mercury from Earth

In earlier times, before spacecraft, we could only see Mercury from Earth as a bright, starlike object. Of the five planets (not counting Earth) that we can see without a telescope, Mercury was probably the last to be discovered. Even with a telescope, it looks small.

When Mercury is nearest Earth, the Sun is on the other side of it. During these times, Earth faces Mercury's nighttime surface. This means we can only see Mercury as a tiny dark disk as it crosses in front of, or transits, the surface of the Sun.

When Mercury is on the other side of the Sun, we <u>could</u> see its day side, except for one problem — the Sun hides it. We can only really see it well when it is to one side of the Sun. Then we see it as a tiny speck.

Our best views of Mercury from telescopes on Earth don't tell us much about the little planet. Even after the Sun sets, Mercury can only be seen through the thickest part of Earth's atmosphere, which blurs the image.

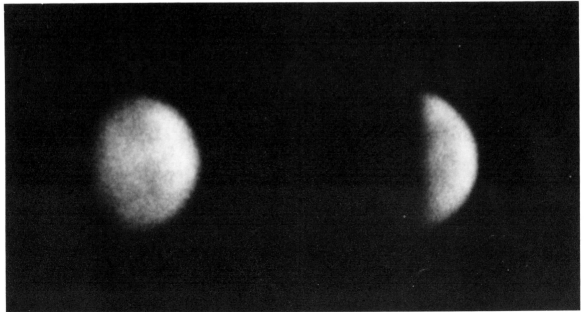

Searching for Mercury

Because Mercury is closer to the Sun than we are, we always see it quite close to the Sun. Most of the time, the Sun's glare makes it impossible to see Mercury. So we should look for it in the eastern sky just before sunrise, or in the western sky just after sunset.

In the evening, Mercury would be visible in the sky for just under an hour or so after the Sun sets. And in the dawn, Mercury would appear in the sky up to just under an hour before the Sun rises. Of course, by the time the Sun rises, our view of Mercury is wiped out.

So if you want to see Mercury, you have to search for it in the twilight or the dawn.

Opposite: Mercury and the crescent Moon. The entire disk of the Moon is dimly visible, illuminated by sunlight reflected from Earth.

Polish astronomer Nicolaus Copernicus, the man who argued that the planets circled around the Sun.

Looking for Mercury — to see or not to see?

Even around sunset or sunrise, Mercury is often so close to the Sun that it is hard to see. The sky is so bright just after sunset or just before sunrise that little Mercury can be missed. In 1543, Polish astronomer Nicolaus Copernicus explained that the planets circle the Sun, not Earth. Even Earth itself circles the Sun. He was one of the most famous astronomers ever, yet the story is that not once in his life did even he manage to catch sight of Mercury. ●

The Myth of Mercury — The Gods' Quick Messenger

The planets are named after ancient gods. Mercury, the messenger of the ancient Roman gods, was usually shown with little wings on his helmet and on his sandals. These showed how rapidly he moved when he was carrying his messages. Because the planet Mercury moves across the sky more rapidly than the other planets, it was named for the speedy messenger of the gods.

Mercury on money. This 1942 US dime is called a Mercury dime. Actually, it shows the goddess of liberty wearing a winged helmet.

Metals were sometimes named for the planets, too. A certain metal looks like silver but is liquid. It was called quicksilver, which means "live silver." Quicksilver was also named for its "quickness" — so it was called "mercury." You've seen this kind of mercury in a thermometer. It's the silver liquid that shows the temperature of you or the world around you.

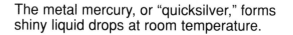

The metal mercury, or "quicksilver," forms shiny liquid drops at room temperature.

Mercury, messenger of the gods.

Quick Mercury —
fast and fooling the ancients

The ancients believed that the faster an object moves across the sky, the nearer to Earth it must be. The Moon moves faster than any other object, so it had to be closest to Earth. They were right about that. But Mercury moves faster than Venus does, so they thought Mercury was closer to Earth than Venus was. Today, we know that Mercury moves as fast as it does because it is near the Sun, not Earth. Venus is closer to Earth than Mercury is.

Albert Einstein, the physicist who explained Mercury's strange movements.

Could an unknown planet explain the odd motion of Mercury? Some astronomers went so far as naming this mystery world after Vulcan, the god of fire.

"Vulcan" — A Modern Myth of Mercury

Mercury moves in its orbit because it is held by the Sun's gravity. The other planets also pull on it slightly. But when all the gravitational pulls were calculated, it turned out that there was a tiny motion of Mercury that couldn't be explained.

Could this motion be caused by the pull of an undiscovered planet even closer to the Sun? For a time, people thought there might be such a planet, and it was called Vulcan, after the god of fire. In more than 50 years of looking, however, no one ever found this planet. Then scientist Albert Einstein worked out a new theory of gravity that accounted for Mercury's odd motion.

The need for a planet like Vulcan had vanished, and so, in the minds of many, did Vulcan!

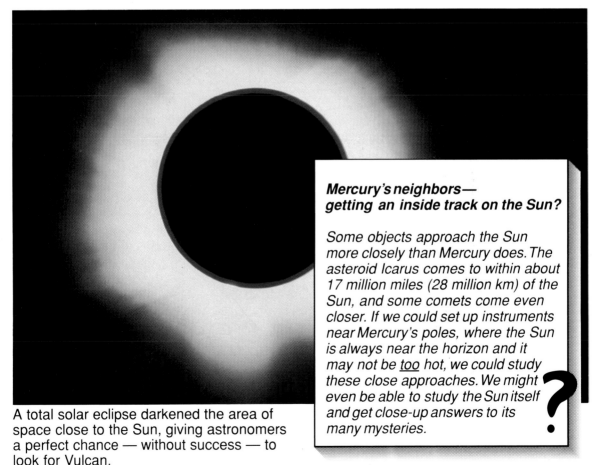

A total solar eclipse darkened the area of space close to the Sun, giving astronomers a perfect chance — without success — to look for Vulcan.

Mercury's neighbors— getting an inside track on the Sun?

Some objects approach the Sun more closely than Mercury does. The asteroid Icarus comes to within about 17 million miles (28 million km) of the Sun, and some comets come even closer. If we could set up instruments near Mercury's poles, where the Sun is always near the horizon and it may not be too hot, we could study these close approaches. We might even be able to study the Sun itself and get close-up answers to its many mysteries.

The Future — Our Key to Mercury's Past

One day, we will send spacecraft back to Mercury. After all, we have mapped less than half of its surface. There might be many interesting things to see on the rest of the Sun's nearest planetary neighbor.

We might like to know more about the cliffs on Mercury, and confirm our theory that they are caused by the planet's shrinking as it cooled off. We have no sign that other rocky worlds, like Venus or the Moon, have been shrinking. So Mercury would give us a chance to study what happens to a planet cooling off when it was formed close to the Sun. We would also like to know more about the interior of Mercury, and whether any quakes occur on Mercury.

Mercury may not be a planet that we would ever think of living on. It's just too close to the Sun. But it would be wonderful to explore more of the <u>inner</u> reaches of our Solar system, as well as its <u>outer</u> reaches. Mercury would be a perfect place to continue that search.

Tiny Mercury — small, but not a lightweight

We used to think Mercury was the smallest planet. Now we know Pluto is even smaller. Even so, Mercury is smaller than some moons. Jupiter's largest moon, Ganymede, and Saturn's largest moon, Titan, are both larger than Mercury. But those moons seem to be made up mainly of icy material, while Mercury is made up of rock and metal. If you could put worlds on a scale, Mercury would weigh more than twice as much as either of those large, icy satellites.

As Mercury's interior cooled and shrank, the surface crust buckled and cracked. Above: an apple's skin wrinkles as the apple dries out and shrinks. Right: part of the fractured Caloris basin on Mercury.

Opposite: A robot lander of the future makes its first study of Mercury's soil.

Fact File: Mercury

Mercury, the closest planet to the Sun, is the eighth largest known planet in our Solar system (Earth is fifth). Only Pluto is smaller. Because Mercury doesn't have an atmosphere, it has no real "weather" as we know it on Earth — only incredibly hot days, and nights just as incredibly cold. Like Venus, Mercury has no moons.

Because Mercury is so hard to see, not much was known about it until the 1960s and 1970s. Since the planet only appeared as a tiny speck that went through phases like the Moon, no one really knew what Mercury's surface was like. But thanks to Mariner 10 and other efforts by scientists to learn more about this planet, we now understand many things about Mercury that were once mysteries. But there's still a lot we would like to know about the "quick planet."

Even if human beings could visit Mercury one day in the future, not many would want to live there. By studying Mercury, however, we can learn a lot about the history of our Solar system — including the part of it where we <u>do</u> live, Earth.

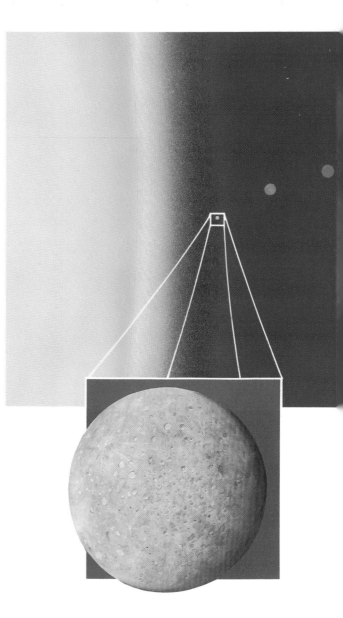

Mercury: How It Measures Up to Earth		
Planet	Diameter	Rotation Period
Mercury	3,030 miles (4,875 km)	58.6 days*
Earth	7,926 miles (12,753 km)	23 hours, 56 minutes

The Sun and Its Family of Planets

Above: The Sun and its Solar system family, left to right: Mercury, Venus, Earth, Mars, Jupiter, Saturn, Uranus, Neptune, Pluto. Left: Here is a close-up of Mercury. Thanks to Mariner 10, we have pictures showing that Mercury's surface is even more heavily cratered than our Moon's.

Period of Orbit Around Sun (length of year)	Moons	Surface Gravity	Distance from Sun (nearest-farthest)	Least Time It Takes for Light to Travel to Earth
88.0 days	0	0.38**	28.5-43.3 million miles (45.9-69.7 million km)	4.4 minutes
365.25 days (one year)	1	1.00**	92-95 million miles (147-152 million km)	

* Mercury rotates, or spins on its axis, once every 58.6 days. It rotates three times for every two trips it makes around the Sun. Because Mercury rotates so slowly, the Sun stays up in Mercury's sky far longer than in Earth's sky. So from Mercury's surface, a solar "day" (sunrise to sunrise) lasts 176 days.
** Multiply your weight by this number to find out how much you would weigh on this planet.

More Books About Mercury

Here are more books that contain information about Mercury. If you are interested in them, check your library or bookstore.

Journey to the Planets. Lauber (Crown)
Our Solar System. Asimov (Gareth Stevens)
The Planets. Couper (Franklin Watts)
The Solar System. Lambert (Franklin Watts)
Wonders Around the Sun. Bonner (Lantern)

Places to Visit

You can explore Mercury and other parts of the Universe without leaving Earth. Here are some museums and centers where you can find a variety of space exhibits.

NASA Langley Research Center
Hampton, Virginia

NASA Lyndon B. Johnson Space Center
Houston, Texas

NASA Lewis Research Center
Cleveland, Ohio

Seneca College Planetarium
North York, Ontario

Dryden Flight Research Center
Edwards, California

Calgary Centennial Planetarium
Calgary, Alberta

Doran Planetarium
Sudbury, Ontario

Hayden Planetarium — Museum of Science
Boston, Massachusetts

For More Information About Mercury

Here are some people you can write to for more information about Mercury. Be sure to tell them exactly what you want to know about or see. Remember to include your age, full name, and address.

For information about Mercury:
The Planetary Society
65 North Catalina
Pasadena, California 91106

STAR DATE
McDonald Observatory
Austin, Texas 78712

Space Communications Branch
Ministry of State for Science and Technology
240 Sparks Street, C. D. Howe Building
Ottawa, Ontario K1A 1A1, Canada

About missions to Mercury:
Alabama Space and Rocket Center
Space Camp Applications
One Tranquility Base
Huntsville, Alabama 35807

NASA Jet Propulsion Laboratory
Public Affairs 180-201
4800 Oak Grove Drive
Pasadena, California 91109

NASA Kennedy Space Center
Educational Services Office
Kennedy Space Center, Florida 32899

For catalogs of slides, posters, and other astronomy materials:
Hansen Planetarium
15 South State Street
Salt Lake City, Utah 84111

Sky Publishing Corporation
49 Bay State Road
Cambridge, Massachusetts 02238-1290

Glossary

asteroid: "star-like"; there are thousands of asteroids in the Solar system, some as very small planets circling the Sun in their own orbits, some as meteoroids, and some possibly as "captured" moons of planets such as Mars.

astronomer: a person involved in the scientific study of the Universe and its various bodies.

atmosphere: the gases that surround a planet, star, or moon.

axis: the imaginary straight line about which a planet, star, or moon turns or spins.

black hole: a massive object — usually a collapsed star — so tightly packed that not even light can escape the force of its gravity.

Copernicus, Nicolaus: a Polish astronomer who was the first to argue that the Sun, not Earth, was the center of our Solar system and that the planets revolved around the Sun.

crater: a hole or pit caused by volcanic explosion or the impact of a meteorite.

Einstein, Albert: a German-born US scientist. His many theories include those concerning unusual motions in a planet's orbit. He is perhaps the best known scientist of the twentieth century.

elliptical: shaped like an oval. Mercury's orbit around the Sun is more elliptical than that of any other planet except Pluto.

fissure: a long, narrow crack, as in a rock or cliff face.

Icarus: an asteroid that approaches the Sun even more closely than Mercury does; named after a mythological boy whose father made him wings of wax and feathers. He flew too close to the Sun and his wings melted, so he tumbled to the sea below.

magnetic field: a field or area around a planet with a center of melted iron — such as Earth. The magnetic field is caused by the planet's rotation, which makes the melted iron in the planet's core swirl. As a result, the planet is like a huge magnet.

orbit: the path that one celestial object follows as it circles, or revolves, around another.

phases: the periods when an object in space is partly or fully lit by the Sun. Like Earth's Moon, Mercury passes through phases as we watch it from Earth.

pole: either end of the axis around which a planet, moon, or star rotates.

probe: a craft that travels in space, photographing celestial bodies and even landing on some of them.

pulsar: a star with all the mass of an ordinary large star but with its mass squeezed into a small ball. It sends out rapid pulses of light or electrical waves.

radiation: the spreading of heat, light, or other forms of energy by rays or waves.

rotate: to turn or spin on an axis.

satellite: a smaller body orbiting a larger body. The Moon is the Earth's natural satellite. Sputnik 1 and 2 were Earth's first artificial satellites.

twilight: the time at sunset when the Sun is below the horizon but there is still a little light left in the sky.

ultraviolet rays: a form of radiation that acts on photographic film and causes burning of your skin in sunshine.

x-rays: a form of radiation that has a shorter wavelength than visible light and can thus pass through materials such as flesh and bones. The shorter its wavelength, the more easily an x-ray passes through a material.

Index

The publishers wish to thank the following for permission to reproduce copyright material: front cover, p. 13,
© Rick Sternbach; pp. 4, 10, 12, 15 (both), 25, 27 (right), photographs courtesy of NASA; p. 5, © Stan
Christensen, courtesy of Beloit Corporation; p. 6, © Pat Rawlings, 1988; p. 7, © Julian Baum, 1988; p. 8, ©
Dorothy Sigler Norton; p. 9, © Lynette Cook, 1988; p. 11 (full page), Jet Propulsion Laboratory; p. 11 (inset),
© Larry Ortiz; p. 14, courtesy of NASA; pp. 16-17, © David A. Hardy; p. 17 (upper left), © MariLynn Flynn,
1987; p. 17 (upper right), © Garret Moore, 1986; p. 18 (both), © Richard Baum, 1988; p. 19, courtesy of New
Mexico State University Observatory; p. 20, © Dennis Milon; pp. 21, 24 (upper), AIP Niels Bohr Library; p. 22
(upper), The Moshe ben Shimon Collection; pp. 22-23 (lower), Matthew Groshek, © Gareth Stevens, Inc.;
pp. 23, 24 (lower), © Keith Ward, 1988; p. 26, © Pamela Lee; p. 27 (center), The University of Chicago
Library; p. 28 (inset), © Sally Bensusen, 1988; pp. 28-29, © Sally Bensusen, 1987.